Claudia,

I know you ____
to read a lot o___
books to get you ___
college degree howeve__
I found one with
lots of great insights
with very few words.
Keep learning...

Lisa

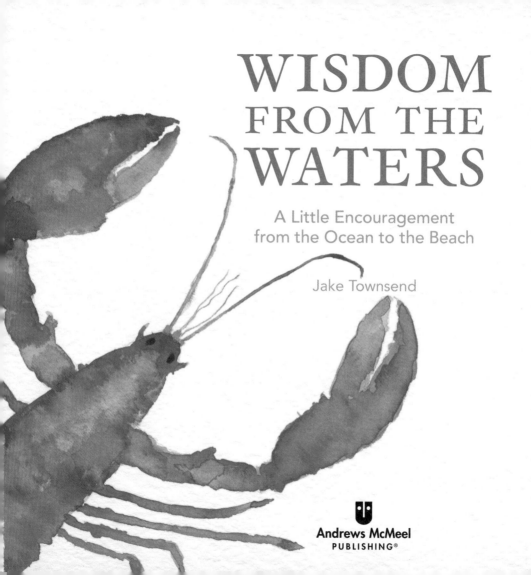

WISDOM
FROM THE
WATERS

A Little Encouragement
from the Ocean to the Beach

Jake Townsend

Andrews McMeel
PUBLISHING®

INTRODUCTION

Whether cetacean or cephalopod, mollusk or mammal, we share our world with the creatures of the waters. For many of us, however, the wonderful animals that populate our vast oceans, our rushing rivers, and our flowing streams are only seen in mere glimpses— flashes of fin and scale, gone as quickly as they came.

What if we spoke the same language?

Imagine what they might tell us.

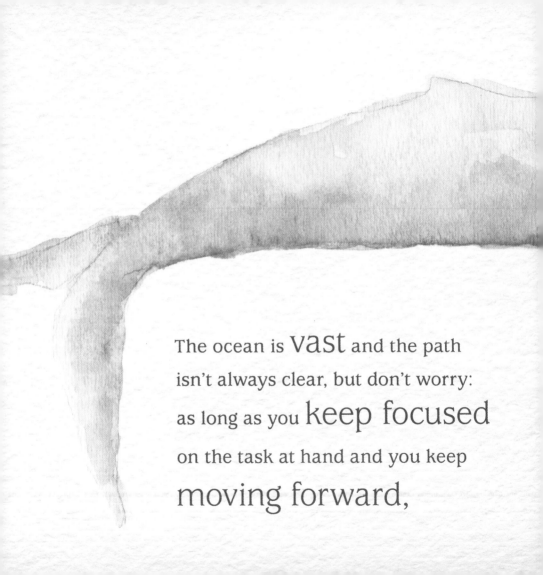

The ocean is vast and the path isn't always clear, but don't worry: as long as you keep focused on the task at hand and you keep moving forward,

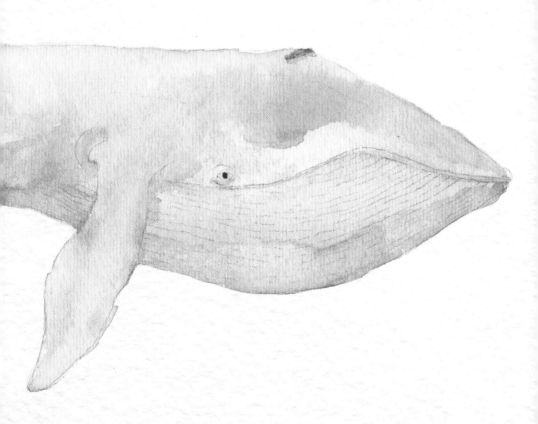

you'll find your way.

A **hard shell** doesn't mean you have a cold heart— be **patient** and **loving** with yourself. You're worth it.

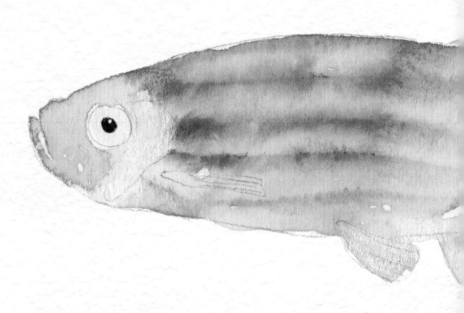

Small ideas can become
big successes.

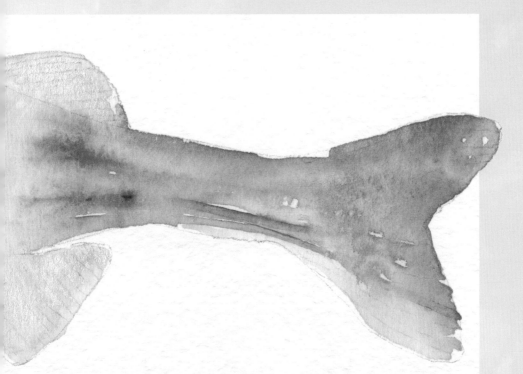

Respect your creativity.

It's true that there is safety in numbers, but sometimes you need to go it alone...

and not feel so safe.

Some of us live between two worlds— life is more interesting that way.

Jump in, the water's fine!

Fear **protects** us from danger, but fear can **keep us from living** our lives.

Be brave.

There's someone

for everyone.

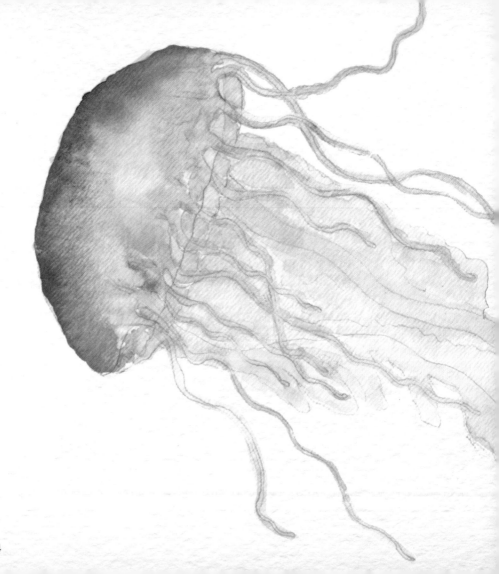

Sometimes it's OK to just
drift for awhile . . .
(but not for too long).

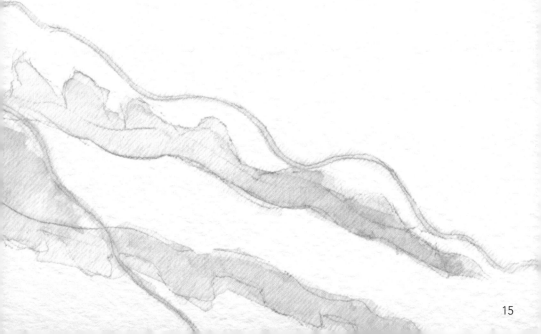

If the water
gets too dark,

rise.

We all get a
little crabby.
(Just try not
to make a
habit of it.)

When you've got
your hands full,
ask for a
little help.

20

Find your own

safe place.

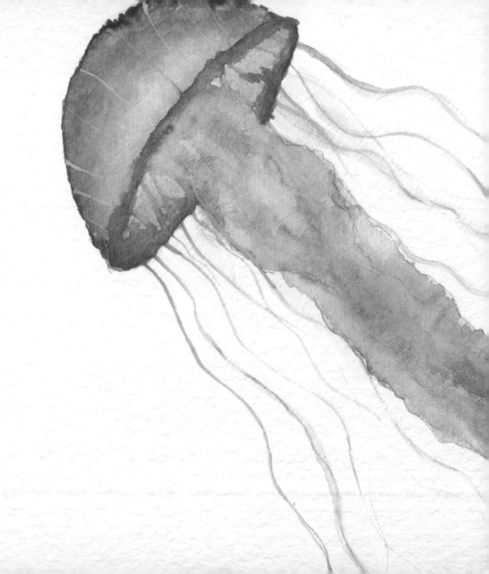

Lasting support comes from within.

Yesterday has passed,
tomorrow hasn't come—
focus on
today.

Take the
plunge.

Keep going.

Sometimes you
have to give
yourself
permission to be
happy.

No one
knows you
better than
you—

ignore the chatter.

Trust your instincts...
you know a lot more than you realize.

No matter how it
may feel,

we are never alone.

Find the **right** school.

Defend yourself

wisely.

Taking charge
of your own life is
important—

44

that's how your

dreams come true,

but resting is just

as important.

Most of the time

it's just your shadow.

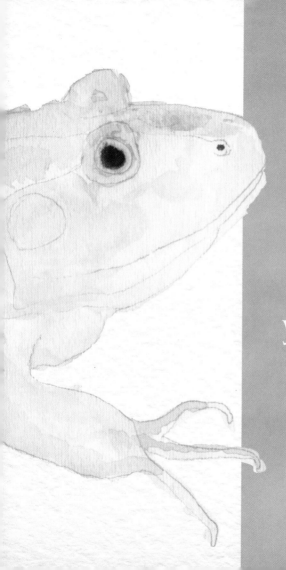

Before
you leap,
observe
for a bit.

It's hard for some of us
to blend in

(lucky us).

Spread
your
fins.

There are times
when you have to

swim upstream.

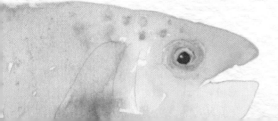

You are never actually stuck. (The solution just hasn't presented itself yet.)

Sit and let your mind wander when you can; it's where your dreams take flight.

The tide **always** turns.

When you hit
the wall,

push
through.

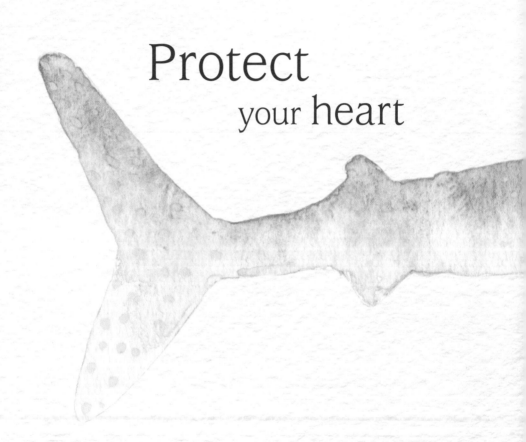

Protect
your heart

(but try to keep it open, too).

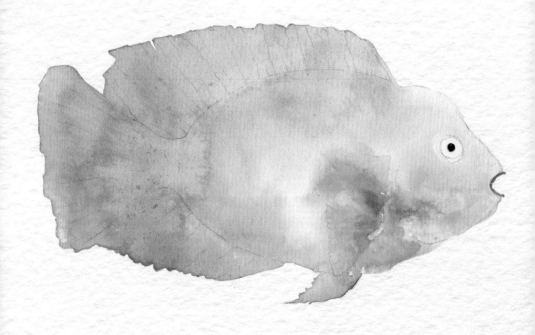

Remind yourself
as many times
as you need to:
I can do this.
I can do this.
I can do this.

Like each drop in an ocean or star in the sky, every one of us has an important place in our world, a place that is rightfully ours.

Honor yours.

But most of all,
no matter what,
keep swimming
and never,
ever give up.

Image key

Blue whale
(Balaenoptera musculus)
A creature without equal, the blue whale is the largest animal known to have ever existed on our planet: adult blue whales can reach lengths up to 100 feet (30 meters) and weigh up to 173 tons. These shy animals usually live alone or with one other whale, and they can hear each other up to 1,000 miles (1,600 kilometers) away.

American lobster
(Homarus americanus)
A native of North America's Atlantic Coast, the American lobster (also known as the Canadian, Maine, or Northern lobster) is the heaviest crustacean in the world's oceans. These sea floor–dwelling marine animals can live 70 years and beyond, reaching sizes of up to 44 pounds (20 kilograms).

Zebrafish
(Danio rerio)
Found in the fresh waters of the Himalayas, the zebrafish was one of the first vertebrates to be cloned. Though its diminutive size would suggest otherwise, seventy percent of human genes have an analogue in zebrafish DNA—making these fish an important research component into the causes of human disease.

Coastal rainbow trout
(Oncorhynchus mykiss irideus)
A member of the salmon family, coastal rainbow trout are native to Pacific Ocean freshwater tributaries along North America's western coast. These colorful fish prefer fresh water but sometimes do end up in the ocean, where they develop silver coloring and take on the name "steelheads."

White's tree frog
(Litoria caerulea)
A highly resilient species, the White's tree frog is known to secrete an infection-pathogen-resistant peptide that is theorized to have aided in protecting the species from decline, unlike many other amphibians. These large frogs have been known to live up to 17 years.

Rainbow darter
(Etheostoma caeruleum)
Native to North America, the rainbow darter is most often seen in swift-moving streams and lakes, and—due to its environmental sensitivity—unpolluted water. This small fish is abundant in the Great Lakes and Ohio River Valley regions of the United States.

Beluga whale
(Delphinapterus leucas)
A highly sociable and vocal cetacean, the beluga whale lives in pods of up to ten individuals, and during the summer season they often gather together to form giant herds of thousands of individuals. The distinctive rounded portion of the head contains the melon, an organ for echolocation.

Atlantic sea nettle
(Chrysaora quinquecirrha)
A common sight in the Atlantic and Indo-Pacific oceans and along the East Coast of the United States, the Atlantic sea nettle is a carnivorous species of jellyfish with a sting that is mildly toxic to humans. Jellyfish are the oldest known multi-organ animal, having been on earth for 700 million years or more.

Southern humpback whale
(Megaptera novaeangliae australis)
Known for their haunting and beautiful underwater vocalization, which can last for hours, humpback whales live in most of the world's oceans. These massive mammals are often seen breaching—they propel more than two-thirds of their bodies above the water before landing back in a splash.

Christmas Island red crab
(Gecarcoidea natalis)
Though it is found only on Australia's Christmas Island in the Indian Ocean, the Christmas Island red crab population is estimated to be more than 100 million. For most of the year, the crabs live alone in secluded forest burrows. However, with the arrival of the wet season from October to November, millions upon millions of these crimson creatures migrate to the ocean for breeding.

East Pacific red octopus
(Octopus rubescens)
A remarkably intelligent and aware being, *Octopus rubescens* was the first invertebrate animal observed to possess an individual personality. As it is with all octopuses, the skin of this creature contains chromatophores that enable it to change color at will.

Blue Crab
(Callinectes sapidus)
Related to lobster and shrimp, blue crabs are bottom-dwellers native to the Gulf of Mexico and the Atlantic Ocean. These ten-legged creatures are adept swimmers and are known to use their sharp pincers if provoked.

Pacific sea nettle
(Chrysaora fuscescens)
Often on display in aquariums, the Pacific sea nettle is found in the coastal oceans along the West Coast of the United States, and less commonly in Japan and the Gulf of Alaska. Though these creatures do not see in the generally understood sense, they can distinguish between light and dark via eyespots, called "ocelli," on their bells and tentacles.

Anemonefish
(Amphiprion ocellaris)
Also known as clownfish, these colorful reef dwellers are recognized by their distinctive orange and white coloring—though some species exhibit pink, black, and red markings. Anemonefish are immune to sea anemone poison and form a symbiotic mutualism with these fellow reef-dwelling animals.

Common bottlenose dolphin
(Tursiops truncatus)
The largest of the beaked dolphins, the common bottlenose dolphin is a highly intelligent, sensitive mammal whose brain is considerably larger than that of humans. Traveling in pods that can include up to 1,000 individuals, these remarkable creatures can swim at speeds exceeding 18 miles per hour and track prey through advanced echolocation.

Bigeye tuna
(Thunnus obesus)
Because their blood has both a high oxygen affinity and efficient oxygen offloading, bigeye tuna are able to closely regulate metabolism in very cold, very deep, low-oxygen ocean depths. The eye for which they are named is unusually large and gives this fish the ability to see in low-light conditions.

Bigfin reef squid
(Sepioteuthis lessoniana)
Sometimes confused with cuttlefish due to its body-length oval fin, the bigfin reef squid is found in the warm waters of the Indian and Pacific Oceans. Due to a combination of structures in the skin called chromatophores, leucophores, and iridophores, this squid species can change skin color and pattern at will.

Red-eyed tree frog
(Agalychnis callidryas)
The red-eyed tree frog is a nonpoisonous, tree-dwelling amphibian native to neotropical forests of Central and South America. During the day, the frogs cover their colorful blue sides and feet by folding their legs into themselves and closing their eyes. The red eyes are theorized to be a defense mechanism meant to startle approaching predators.

Sperm whale
(Physeter macrocephalus)
The sperm whale is the largest toothed predator on earth and one of the loudest; its clicking vocalization can reach levels of 230 decibels. This enormous mammal, which can grow to lengths of 67 feet (20 meters), possesses the largest brain of any animal—its head alone accounts for nearly one-third of its body length. Ambergris, a waste material from the whale's digestive tract, is a prized ingredient in perfume.

Tiger tail seahorse
(Hippocampus comes)
Named for its distinctly horse-like appearance, the seahorse is one of the only fish species that is monogamous for life. After an elaborate mating ritual that resembles a coordinated dance, the female deposits her eggs into the male's pouch where he gestates them until the fully developed seahorse young emerge.

Pyramid butterflyfish
(Hemitaurichthys polylepis)
A native of the Indo-Pacific Ocean, the pyramid butterfly-fish is often found in the outer reef slopes, where it can find shelter after venturing into the deeper open waters of its tropical territory to feed. These fish, like most of the species in the Chaetodontidae family, form pairs that stake out and defend a chosen coral head.

Indo-Pacific sailfish
(Istiophorus platypterus)
This species of billfish lives in the warmer oceans around the world. Growing to lengths of nearly 5 feet (1.5 meters), adults can reach speeds of 47 miles per hour (75 kilometers per hour)—one of the highest recorded speeds of any aquatic animal.

Northern green frog, royal variety
(Lithobates clamitans melanota regilus)
A native to North America, this royal frog is often found on the shores of freshwater lakes and streams. Active day and night, this type of frog is one of only five species of frog in the Americas with a presently reigning royal family. The individual depicted here is the current king.

Chinook salmon
(Oncorhynchus tshawytscha)
These prized fish are found in both fresh and salt water, spend-ing an average of three years in the ocean before returning to their home fresh waters to spawn. When returning from the ocean, Chinooks lose their silvery color and, in males, develop a hook in the jaw called a "kype."

European common frog
(Rana temporaria)
Though usually ranging in hues from olive to brown, the Euro-pean common frog can lighten or darken the color of its skin at will in order to better camouflage itself for safety. Found throughout Europe and Scandinavia, this semiaquatic frog species has a transparent inner eyelid, allowing it to see in water.

Yelloweye rockfish
(Sebastes ruberrimus)
Also known as the red snapper, which is not the same as the species of warm-water fish also known as "red snapper," the yelloweye rockfish is the longest-living fish species in the world, with individuals recorded to have lived to 120 years of age.

Killer whale
(Orcinus orca)
An apex predator, the killer whale has no immediate foe. Orcas are highly intelligent and social animals; they often live in matrilineal pods, which are considered to be the most stable social groups of any communal animal. Orcas are the largest dolphin species and can live as long as 59 years in the wild.

Cutthroat trout
(Oncorhynchus clarkii)
A North American native, the cutthroat trout is found in the cold waters of the Rockies, the Great Basin, and the Pacific Ocean. This subspecies of Pacific trout was first recorded by European explorers in the American Southwest in 1541.

Veiltail goldfish
(Carassius auratus)
The veiltail is a type of goldfish that is characterized by its flowing double tail and prominent dorsal fin. This unique fish is the result of crossbreeding a Japanese ryukin goldfish with a telescope eye goldfish. Goldfish are in the carp family; their coloring is the result of an early mutation.

Brown crab
(Cancer pagurus)
Commonly found in the waters of the North Atlantic Ocean and the North Sea, the brown crab is a relatively abundant marine creature. The average lifespan is 25 to 30 years, though some brown crabs have recorded lifespans of up to 100 years.

Lyretail anthias
(Pseudanthias squamipinnis)
Found in the oceans of Fiji, Indonesia, and Vanuatu, the lyretail anthias is a social animal that lives in large schools around coral reefs. This brightly colored marine fish is hermaphroditic; if the dominant male of a group is no longer present, the dominant female will become male and assume the lead.

Narwhal
(Monodon monoceros)
The tusk that characterizes the narwhal is actually a canine tooth that extends from the left side of the upper jaw, though about 1 in 500 narwhals have two tusks protruding from either side of the jaw. The tusk is a sensing organ believed to collect information from the water.

Whale shark
(Rhincodon typus)
A true gentle giant, the whale shark—the largest non-mammalian animal in the world—is a docile creature that feeds on plankton and small fish. It is the largest fish in the sea, with some individuals reaching lengths of 40 feet (12 meters) or more. They are believed to have lifespans that average 70 to 100 years.

Midas cichlid
(Amphilophus citrinellus)
A native to the freshwater lakes and rivers of Central America, the Midas cichlid (which is actually a trade name) is a resilient and territorial fish. The protrusion on the head, called a nuchal hump, is present in both males and females, though the male nuchal hump is usually larger.

North Pacific humpback whale
(Megaptera novaeangliae kuzira)
A native of the North Pacific Ocean, the North Pacific humpback is one of three subspecies of this magnificent mammal, and it is characterized by a darker hue on the upper flipper. The nodules on humpbacks' heads, called "tubercules," are sensory organs akin to whiskers on a cat.

Andrews McMeel Publishing
a division of Andrews McMeel Universal
1130 Walnut Street, Kansas City, Missouri 64106

www.andrewsmcmeel.com

17 18 19 20 21 SDB 10 9 8 7 6 5 4 3 2 1

ISBN: 978-1-4494-8714-0

Library of Congress Control Number: 2017932228

Editor: Patty Rice
Designer, Art Director: Julie Barnes
Production Editor: Erika Kuster
Production Manager: Tamara Haus

ATTENTION: SCHOOLS AND BUSINESSES
Andrews McMeel books are available at quantity discounts with
bulk purchase for educational, business, or sales promotional use.
For information, please e-mail the Andrews McMeel Publishing
Special Sales Department: specialsales@amuniversal.com.